Little RIDDLERS

Essex Verses

Edited By Machaela Gavaghan

First published in Great Britain in 2018 by:

Young Writers
Remus House
Coltsfoot Drive
Peterborough
PE2 9BF
Telephone: 01733 890066
Website: www.youngwriters.co.uk

All Rights Reserved
Book Design by Ashley Janson
© Copyright Contributors 2018
SB ISBN 978-1-78896-772-3
Printed and bound in the UK by BookPrintingUK
Website: www.bookprintinguk.com
YB0372D

FOREWORD

Dear Reader,

Are you ready to get your thinking caps on to puzzle your way through this wonderful collection?

Young Writers' Little Riddlers competition set out to encourage young writers to create their own riddles. Their answers could be whatever or whoever their imaginations desired; from people to places, animals to objects, food to seasons. Riddles are a great way to further the children's use of poetic expression, including onomatopoeia and similes, as well as encourage them to 'think outside the box' by providing clues without giving the answer away immediately.

All of us here at Young Writers believe in the importance of inspiring young children to produce creative writing, including poetry, and we feel that seeing their own riddles in print will keep that creative spirit burning brightly and proudly.

We hope you enjoy riddling your way through this book as much as we enjoyed reading all the entries.

CONTENTS

Boxted St Peter's CE Primary School, Boxted

Crystal-Jo Harding (6)	1
Evie Grace MacRae (7)	2
Henry Hopkins (7)	3
Summer Woodgate (7)	4

Burrsville Community Infant School, Clacton-On-Sea

Millie Rose Hipkin (6)	5

Glade Primary School, Clayhall

Michelle Diaku (6)	6
Riddhi Agarwal (6)	7

Ingatestone Infant School, Ingatestone

Bailey Denham (7)	8
Owen Hicks (7)	10
Sophie Finlay (7)	12
Alana-Rose Tubby (7)	14
Joana Y Matayoshi de Oliveira (7)	16
William Taylor (6)	18
Luca Buck (6)	19
Finn Saunders (7)	20
Joshua England (7)	22
Lewis James Evans (7)	24
Evan Victor Donnell (7)	25
Finley Gunning (7)	26
Reuben Finn (7)	27
Lauren Odukogbe (7)	28
Lilly Wheeler (7)	29

Harry Edward Young (7)	30
Vien Pamiloza (7)	31
Benjamin McArthur (6)	32
Zoë Carmichael (7)	33
Jessica Louise Dale (7)	34
Christopher Beecher (7)	35
Natalie Allen (7)	36
Lucas Taylor (6)	37
Dominic Westgate (7)	38
Thomas Donno (6)	39
Alex Cavanagh (7)	40
Scarlett Finch-Hutchins (7)	41
James Farrow (7)	42

John Perry Primary School, Dagenham

Bethany Alexandra Hill (6)	43
Ammar-Yusuf Mohd Aswat (7)	44
Dominykas Boczek (7)	45
Ranad Shereif (6)	46
Jasmine Marie Bell (7)	47
Dominykas Zabulis (7)	48
Simonas Gudas (7)	49
Neitanas Miliauskis (7)	50
Khairah Ahmed (7)	51
Ibrahim Abdur-Rahman (7)	52
Daniel Adegoke (7)	53
Ava Olivia Phillips (6)	54
Kai Turner (7)	55
Alex Robert Dickens (7)	56
Ekaterina Skolska (6)	57
Chibumnuche Oprah-Gorgeous Eneremadu (7)	58
Shazneen Haque (7)	59
Lewis Bivens (7)	60

Sara Beiene (6)	61
Daniel Onyedikachukwu Obeigue (7)	62
Valerie Rua Gutierrez (6) & Victor	63
Shannon Thapa (7)	64
Mia Christie (6)	65
Madison Rose (7)	66
Melis Adan (7)	67
Brendan Bowen (7)	68
Keziah Pothin (8)	69
Krystal Lacuna Bird (6)	70
Emily Maria Lungu (6)	71
Abdullah Burki (7)	72
Kian David Asamoah (6)	73
Alexandra Afolayan (7)	74
Michael Okinbaloye (7)	75
Nifemi Esho (6)	76
Elze Zabulyte (7)	77
Ronnie Peter Keith Bland (7)	78
Rdwan Montasir (6)	79
Ifechukwu Joshua Anuna (6)	80
Samuel Elijah (7)	81
Ronnie Spence (7)	82

Newtons Primary School, Rainham

Spencer Garcia (6)	83
Ruby Reed (6)	84
Anton Gabriel (5)	85
Ellie Wicks (6)	86
Robert John Wisbey (6)	87
Max Turner (6)	88
Grace Gibbons (6)	89
Lillie Davenport (5)	90
Rehnuma Tajrin (5)	91
Zara Kasule (6)	92
Laila Tonto (6)	93
James Hammond (6)	94
Alfie Feasey (6)	95
William Mason (6)	96
Lilly-Rose Bailey (5)	97
Naya Garcia-Clegg (5)	98

Bobby Potter (6)	99
Kiah Morris (6)	100
Amy Rodriguez-Ahmed (6)	101
Rabiah Azhar (5)	102
Samanta Smeiksta (5)	103
Bailey George Kreuder (6)	104
Jay-J Gardiner (5)	105
Katie Davenport (5)	106
Lilly-Rose Persia Akbari (6)	107
Amber Debenham (5)	108
Bryan Buttery (6)	109

Whybridge Infant School, Rainham

Nifise Femi-Sanni (7)	110
Elsie-Lennox Morgan (7)	111
Kirsten Asante (6)	112
Tiana Tu (7)	113
Jessica Denise Middleton Marden (7)	114
Noah Ashaley Leach (7)	115
Dovydas Zilionis (6)	116
Declan Armstrong-Smith (7)	117
Seyi Odukaya (7)	118
Bobby Fletcher (7)	119
Yasir Uddin (7)	120
Kaden Sydes (7)	121
Richard Bogdan Gavrau (6)	122
Liam Breavington (6)	123
Ellie Cox (6)	124
Marta Jurga (7)	125
Ekisha Kaiza (7)	126
Katie Weston-Lucas (7)	127
Albos Dega (7)	128
Vinny Joseph Kerrigan (7)	129
Jack Barry (7)	130
Hollie Hartley (7)	131
Connor Mason Ross (7)	132
Aironas Astrauskas (7)	133
Mia Ramanauskaite (7)	134
Jonny Melhuish (7)	135
Honey-Blue Donoghue (6)	136
Jake Flatt (7)	137

Ethan Micheal Clifton (7)	138
Solange Danso (7)	139
Luca Greenspan (6)	140
Caiden Sita (6)	141
Charlie Harris (7)	142
Teddy Snee (6)	143
Altay Kocak (7)	144
Ioana Dainty (7)	145
Leo Foster (7)	146
Olivia Jackson (7)	147
Georgia Turner (7)	148
Dilanas Bogusa (7)	149
Nikola Bojdzińska (7)	150
Simon Olabisi (7)	151
Joan Ukpokolo (7)	152
Jake Charlie Tony Walker (6)	153
Kaiden Linford-Mehmet (7)	154
Riley Chuch (7)	155
Izhonia Romewun Pearl Agbaje (6)	156

THE POEMS

The Graceful Swimmer

I come in all different shapes and sizes.
I have a long, wavy tail and fins.
They help me swim in my home.
My eyes are big.
My scales are shiny and shimmer
in the blue sea.
What am I?

Answer: A fish.

Crystal-Jo Harding (6)
Boxted St Peter's CE Primary School, Boxted

What Am I?

I like to chase a ball or fetch a stick.
I have a wet, shiny nose.
I have four legs and four paws.
I sleep in a bed or a basket.
I eat and drink from a bowl.
I like to bark.
What am I?

Answer: A dog.

Evie Grace MacRae (7)
Boxted St Peter's CE Primary School, Boxted

Ruler

I had a pet lion and 103 children.
My home was near the River Nile.
I ruled for sixty-six years and I believed in many gods.
When I died, I was buried in a pyramid.
Who am I?

Answer: Ramesses the Great.

Henry Hopkins (7)
Boxted St Peter's CE Primary School, Boxted

Crack Me Open!

I am round,
I am brown,
You can find me up high or on the ground.
I am hairy,
Crack me open and I am juicy,
I am tasty with no wastie.
What am I?

Answer: A coconut.

Summer Woodgate (7)
Boxted St Peter's CE Primary School, Boxted

Frosty Feet

They eat smelly fish.
They have big wings.
They can live on the sandy beach.
They have no sharp teeth.
They cannot fly with colourful birds.
They stay in big, noisy groups.
What are they?

Answer: Penguins.

Millie Rose Hipkin (6)
Burrsville Community Infant School, Clacton-On-Sea

Precious Me

I am always watery.
I have a lid but I am not a pot.
Nearly every species on the planet
has a pair of me.
I follow things everywhere.
I am very important in a human body.
I always get scared when
suddenly approached.
What am I?

Answer: An eye.

Michelle Diaku (6)
Glade Primary School, Clayhall

My Birthday Gift!

I am transport.
I go on the road.
People sit on me
To go to places to see.
I am red.
I don't eat bread.
What am I?

Answer: A bus.

Riddhi Agarwal (6)
Glade Primary School, Clayhall

A Healthy Snack

I'm a vegetable.
I don't need to be peeled.
My skin is very smooth and usually,
I'm white.
My type usually grows in many places:
Forests, rainforests, jungles
and sometimes gardens.
My type comes in many different colours:
White, green, red, blue, purple, orange
and sometimes I glow!
Don't touch me, I can be dangerous
and poisonous.
Some types of me aren't poisonous.
You can eat me or use me to flavour food
but I'm not saying all my type are edible!
If you eat a poisonous type of me,
you can be badly injured or very ill.
The best place to get me is in a shop.

I don't give lots of taste or flavour.
My type is umbrella-shaped.
Did you know that I can also be multicoloured as well?
What am I?

Answer: A mushroom.

Bailey Denham (7)
Ingatestone Infant School, Ingatestone

A Healthy Snack

I am a vegetable full of slime.
If you feel me, I am smooth.
Don't forget to wash me, I grow on mud.
I am as white as snow.
My size is bigger than a pea
and smaller than a melon.
My seeds are under my bump on top of me.
Sometimes we come in all shapes and sizes.
My colours are blue, white, yellow, purple
and multicoloured.
Sometimes if you eat me,
I might taste slimy.
I am used to make soup.
You'll have to check me before eating me
because I might be poisonous.
Did you know that I can glow in the dark?
The place that I normally grow in is damp.
Some of us grow very slowly or very quickly.

I am shaped like an umbrella.
What am I?

Answer: A mushroom.

Owen Hicks (7)
Ingatestone Infant School, Ingatestone

A Healthy Snack

I am a fruit.
Inside me I have very soft flesh.
Remember to peel me before you eat me!
The colour of me is a yellowy-green colour.
I change colour as I ripen.
My skin is very fuzzy and at the top of me
it is very prickly.
I am extremely sweet, juicy and delicious.
You can make me into jelly and juice
or a colourful fruit salad.
People can find me in hot countries
like Spain and Egypt.
My shape is usually an oval but my top
is amazingly spiky and long.
Did you know if you plant me in the soil,
another one of me will grow?

I am bigger than an apple but smaller than a watermelon.
What am I?

Answer: A pineapple.

Sophie Finlay (7)
Ingatestone Infant School, Ingatestone

A Healthy Snack

I am a fruit.
When you bite into me, you'll taste
the sweet, tasty juice inside and outside.
My skin makes a funny noise
when you scrape your finger on me.
Make sure you wash me carefully
before you eat me.
I am full of yumminess and tastiness.
You could have me as a drink
and with your breakfast.
I am bigger than a grape
but smaller than a banana.
I feel crunchy when you eat me.
Sometimes I can be red,
sometimes I can be green.
When I am mouldy, you can't eat me.

Did you know my seeds are the shape of raindrops?
What am I?

Answer: An apple.

Alana-Rose Tubby (7)
Ingatestone Infant School, Ingatestone

A Healthy Snack

I am a fruit.
My colour is a light, bumpy orange colour.
You can make jam and juice from me.
If you go to hot places, you might see me up in a tree.
Loads of people eat me for lunch, breakfast and dinner.
I am the shape of a sphere.
If you don't use me for a long time,
my skin will get wrinkly and hard.
I taste juicy and sometimes sour.
You can pull my skin with your fingers.
Did you know there are ten segments inside of me?
I am bigger than a blueberry

but smaller than a pineapple.
What am I?

Answer: An orange.

Joana Y Matayoshi de Oliveira (7)
Ingatestone Infant School, Ingatestone

My Favourite Minibeast

I'm bigger than a ladybird
but smaller than a bird.
I don't have legs, hands and bones.
I'm a very useful creature because
I help plants grow.
You will find me in the grass or fields.
When you look at me,
I'm pink, soft and smooth.
I like to wriggle and dig underground.
Don't step on me because I will die!
Don't you know I have to always be wet?
I like to eat soil and dead plants.
When it is raining, I come to the surface
so you can see me.
I breathe through my skin.
What am I?

Answer: A worm.

William Taylor (6)
Ingatestone Infant School, Ingatestone

Little Riddlers 2018 - Essex Verses

My Favourite Animal

I move very fast.
I am very good at hiding.
I am very small.
I am bigger than an ant
but smaller than an elephant.
First I start in an egg.
My armour is to protect me from danger.
If you see me, I will be as shiny as gold.
If you see me, I am shiny blue.
Don't squash me because I will die!
Don't rip my wings because they are delicate.
When you are looking for me, you will find me in the colourful, beautiful garden.
What am I?

Answer: A blue beetle.

Luca Buck (6)
Ingatestone Infant School, Ingatestone

A Healthy Snack

I am a fruit.
My colour is as red as a postbox.
You don't need to peel me and cook me.
When you eat me, I'm juicy
and full of goodness.
I am extremely and amazingly smooth.
My shape is a round sphere.
In the summertime, I'm most popular.
Don't eat me when I'm green
because I am not ready.
I grow on plants.
The size of me is bigger than a seed
but smaller than an apple.
Did you know you can make me
into ketchup?

I have a green, spiky and smooth stalk. What am I?

Answer: A tomato.

Finn Saunders (7)
Ingatestone Infant School, Ingatestone

My Favourite Minibeast

I am a minibeast.
My life starts as a white, round egg
on a leaf.
I live in many places:
gardens, farms and parks.
Mostly, I eat aphids and leaves.
I drink sometimes.
I am bigger than an ant
but smaller than a butterfly.
If you listen, I am silent.
To move I can fly but I can walk.
Be extremely careful so you don't
squash me!
I can be red, black, orange and yellow.
Do you know I'm a type of beetle?

Mostly, I am red with spots on.
What am I?

Answer: A ladybird.

Joshua England (7)
Ingatestone Infant School, Ingatestone

My Favourite Animal

I am an animal.
You can find me in a forest.
I am smaller than a bear,
but bigger than a fish.
When you look at me, I am black and white.
Don't go near because you can scare me!
Beware of my claws, I might scratch you.
I started as an egg
and then went into a cub.
I am beautiful, wonderful and delightful
and so soft.
Did you know that I am so nice?
Did you know I only eat bamboo leaves?
You can also find me in a zoo.
What am I?

Answer: A panda.

Lewis James Evans (7)
Ingatestone Infant School, Ingatestone

A Fantastic Insect

I am an insect.
When I am born, I have 200 brothers
and sisters.
My dinner is insects but I am not a spider.
Bigger than a grain of salt
but smaller than a fingernail.
Don't look for me at Christmas because
I am hibernating at that time.
If you look in your shed, you might see me.
To move my legs, I do a rowing action.
I have a small head and big eyes.
With a glide and a hop,
I'm speeding across the water.
What am I?

Answer: A pond skater.

Evan Victor Donnell (7)
Ingatestone Infant School, Ingatestone

Fourth Favourite Pokémon

I am a ghost-type shadow ball and dark.
I can use Shadow Ball and Nightmare.
If you go near me,
I will bite you with my fangs!
I live in a haunted mansion
that is very creepy.
I am a basic type.
If you touch me, you will have a nightmare.
I am purple and black.
Don't touch me,
I will burn you with my ghost fire!
I am dangerous, I am not friendly!
I am a Pokémon.
I am powerful because I can mega evolve!
Who am I?

Answer: Gastly.

Finley Gunning (7)
Ingatestone Infant School, Ingatestone

A Healthy Fruit

I am a fruit full of vitamins.
Some people make me into a smoothie.
When you eat me, I'm soft, creamy
and light green.
The colour of me is dark green.
If you touch me, I am hard and rippled.
In the middle of me, I have a stone.
My size is bigger than a grape
but smaller than a melon.
I am the shape of a snowman.
You need to peel me before you eat me.
The place you find me is high up
in the trees in Mexico.
What am I?

Answer: An avocado.

Reuben Finn (7)
Ingatestone Infant School, Ingatestone

A Healthy Snack

I am a fruit.
I am dark red.
Sometimes I grow on a fruit farm
with all my friends.
I am bigger than grapes
but smaller than apples.
You can use me to make jam
and smoothies too.
When you eat me, I am full of goodness
and I'll make you happy and smile.
I can be used to make fruit salad.
Don't forget to wash me very well!
You can see me with all my family.
Did you know I belong to the rose family?
What am I?

Answer: A cherry.

Lauren Odukogbe (7)
Ingatestone Infant School, Ingatestone

A Healthy Snack

If you touch me, I feel smooth, squashy
and my stone is brown and hard.
I am a fruit.
I am bigger than an ant
and smaller than a pineapple.
Be careful if you squeeze me,
I can go in your eye!
I grow on a beautiful green tree.
You can make delicious crumbles with me.
My taste is sweet, juicy and yummy.
Normally I am red or a purple colour.
Don't swallow the pip because
I can get stuck in your throat.
What am I?

Answer: A cherry.

Lilly Wheeler (7)
Ingatestone Infant School, Ingatestone

A Minibeast

I am an insect.
First I start as a shiny, smooth egg.
Mostly, I am smaller than a butterfly
but bigger than an ant.
My favourite drink is sweet, sticky nectar.
When you see my fuzzy body, you can see
my stripy brown and orange blocks.
If you go into the garden, you might
hear my extremely loud buzzing.
Be careful you do not tread on me!
Did you know amazingly, I flap my wings
200 times a second?
What am I?

Answer: A bumblebee.

Harry Edward Young (7)
Ingatestone Infant School, Ingatestone

My Favourite Minibeast

When my life starts, I am in a small, shiny egg.
I am a minibeast.
I live in forests, gardens, parks and fields.
I eat aphids, they are very juicy!
To move, I walk and fly.
My colour is red and black.
Sometimes I have orange and black spots.
Some of us are poisonous.
Be careful, you might step on me
and I'm extremely delicate.
I am smaller than a ball
but I am bigger than an ant.
What am I?

Answer: A ladybird.

Vien Pamiloza (7)
Ingatestone Infant School, Ingatestone

A Healthy Snack

I am a fruit.
If you see me, I am dark red.
When you see me growing, I am on a tree.
I start as a blossom, my stalk is green.
I am bigger than an ant
but smaller than a grape.
People can use me to make
colourful jam and juice.
If you feel me, I feel smooth.
My taste is normally extremely sweet,
however, sometimes sour.
Did you know, if you try to eat my stone
you might choke?
What am I?

Answer: A cherry.

Benjamin McArthur (6)
Ingatestone Infant School, Ingatestone

A Healthy Snack

I am a fruit.
If you touch me I might be quite hard.
When you look carefully, I've got green skin
with light red, juicy insides.
Try biting into me, you might think
I am extremely juicy, soft and delicious.
I am bigger than an apple
but smaller than a child's coat.
My shape is an oval,
just like the shape of an egg.
Mostly I grow in hot countries
and low to the ground.
What am I?

Answer: A watermelon.

Zoë Carmichael (7)
Ingatestone Infant School, Ingatestone

A Healthy Snack

I am a fruit.
Inside me I have seeds.
The colour of me is red.
I am bigger than a raisin
and smaller than a pear.
The shape of me is round.
Also, I am used to make other things.
If you eat me,
you will need to wash me first.
I am soft and smooth.
I grow on farms.
My taste is extremely juicy.
Did you know in 2013, there was one of me grown that weighed 3.51kg in America?
What am I?

Answer: A tomato.

Jessica Louise Dale (7)
Ingatestone Infant School, Ingatestone

My Second Favourite Animal

I am an animal.
I live in Antarctica.
I am cute, fluffy and kind.
The size of me is bigger than an ant but smaller than a car.
Don't go near me, I will kick you!
I swim in the water.
I am white, black and orange.
If you see me, I could be swimming to catch fish.
I start as an egg and turn into a chick.
I have flippers to walk and swim.
The feathers on me are soft.
What am I?

Answer: A penguin.

Christopher Beecher (7)
Ingatestone Infant School, Ingatestone

A Minibeast

I am a minibeast.
My life starts as a shiny, beautiful egg.
All my species are completely silent
when we move.
I live in gardens, parks and meadows.
For my food, I love to eat delicious aphids.
I am a part of the beetle family.
Look out because you could squash me.
Did you know
there are many different types of me?
I am usually red but I can be yellow
or orange.
What am I?

Answer: A ladybird.

Natalie Allen (7)
Ingatestone Infant School, Ingatestone

A Special Object

I'm an object.
I'm soft and squashy.
Don't eat me, I'm not a food!
I can be any colour like white, green
and yellow.
When you look at me, I'm bigger than a bird
but smaller than a book.
I am helpful because I suck up water
but I'm not a sponge.
Do you know you can find me
in the kitchen or the bathroom?
You can also find me in the garage.
What am I?

Answer: Foam.

Lucas Taylor (6)
Ingatestone Infant School, Ingatestone

My Second Favourite Pokémon

I'm a Pokémon and I'm an electric
and normal type.
My speed is faster than a sports car
but slower than a cheetah.
I'm smaller than an elephant
but bigger than a bug.
If you look at me, I am brown and yellow.
If you wake me up, I will zap you.
I live on a Pokémon farm.
Sometimes I might charge.
Sometimes I might bite.
Who am I?

Answer: Tauros.

Dominic Westgate (7)
Ingatestone Infant School, Ingatestone

My Favourite Animal

I'm an animal.
I'm more powerful than a lion.
I'm as soft as a cat.
I'm spotty and yellow and stripy.
I have sharp teeth and claws.
Don't go near me because I might eat you!
I'm scary, sneaky and I move very quickly.
I live in a hot country.
I am badly behaved when I see a person.
I live in Africa.
What am I?

Answer: A cheetah.

Thomas Donno (6)
Ingatestone Infant School, Ingatestone

My Favourite Minibeast

I have four wings and four legs.
You can find me near ponds.
I am bigger than a wasp
but smaller than a worm.
My wings are beautiful,
bright and transparent.
Don't touch my wings because
they are delicate.
Listen for my hum.
Don't worry, I won't breathe fire!
What am I?

Answer: A dragonfly.

Alex Cavanagh (7)
Ingatestone Infant School, Ingatestone

My Favourite Animal

I am an animal that lives in the woods.
I eat rabbits.
I have a bushy tail.
I also eat fish.
Be careful, I might bite!
The size of me is medium.
Did you know that I have night vision?
I come out at night.
I get up to find food.
I am orange and red.
What am I?

Answer: A fox.

Scarlett Finch-Hutchins (7)
Ingatestone Infant School, Ingatestone

A Special Animal

I am a big predator to fish.
I need to go under the water.
When you see me, I look bright blue.
I eat fish.
I am bigger than a tree.
I am under the ground.
I have a long head and body.
I don't eat meat, I only eat fish.
What am I?

Answer: A dinosaur.

James Farrow (7)
Ingatestone Infant School, Ingatestone

The Fluffiest Pet

I sprint so my predator doesn't catch me
so I don't get eaten.
I'm the only animal in the world
who can jump the highest.
Sometimes I can be wild,
sometimes I am not.
When I hear something coming,
I run in my safe hutch.
I eat juicy carrots and I nibble them all up.
If you touch me, I will be scared but
if I am your pet, I will be the happiest thing.
What am I?

Answer: A rabbit.

Bethany Alexandra Hill (6)
John Perry Primary School, Dagenham

Dark Predator

I'm bigger than a tiny grasshopper
but smaller than a terrifying shark.
I run on my paws with my sharp claws.
When I go *grrr*, I am angry
because I can't catch my enemies.
My fur is as furry as a tiger and a cat.
My teeth are as sharp as a knife
and I might bite your head off.
Also, you might know me because
I'm a Marvel superhero.
What am I?

Answer: A black panther.

Ammar-Yusuf Mohd Aswat (7)
John Perry Primary School, Dagenham

Jungle Predator

I am smaller than a colossal lion
but I am bigger than a buzzing bee.
I sneak up on my delicious prey with my four
mini paws and then I gobble them up!
I am as gentle as possible
but if you're not gentle, I'll bite you!
I am not a good pet at all
because I have sharp teeth.
Also, I live in a jungle.
I have a smooth tail, just don't step on it!
What am I?

Answer: An ocelot.

Dominykas Boczek (7)
John Perry Primary School, Dagenham

Waddle Waddle

I am bigger than a tiny ant but I am
smaller than a huge, grey elephant.
I waddle on my wet, webbed feet
and I love to splash in the fresh water.
When I am happy, I quack.
When I dip into the freezing river,
I come out as if I was drenched in rain!
Some of my family are famous.
Do you know someone called Ugly?
What am I?

Answer: A duck.

Ranad Shereif (6)
John Perry Primary School, Dagenham

Scaliest Animal

When you touch me,
I will move very speedily.
My skin feels gooey, inky and disgusting.
I am very motionless and sneaky.
I'll creep up on you
and act like a rock and camouflage.
I move slowly like a queen.
Sometimes I'm stubborn
like an angry hyena.
I can't wait to be your pet!
What am I?

Answer: A lizard.

Jasmine Marie Bell (7)
John Perry Primary School, Dagenham

What Am I?

I am as solid as a statue
but as big as a palace.
I am made of grey stone and I cannot move.
Sometimes I might creak but I don't talk.
I can feel as hot as the burning sun
and as cold as an ice block.
I have lots of rooms with big glass windows
and a large garden with colourful trees.
What am I?

Answer: A mansion.

Dominykas Zabulis (7)
John Perry Primary School, Dagenham

Slimy Waves

All the time, I'm slower than a sloth.
I eat sea snails and I'm black and green.
I'm very silent, sneaky and I camouflage in the dark.
I'm as slimy as water.
I'm very soft.
People think I'm disgusting.
I try to hide from people because they attack me.
What am I?

Answer: A sea cucumber.

Simonas Gudas (7)
John Perry Primary School, Dagenham

What Am I?

I am bigger than a baby fly
but I am smaller than a dog.
I have three tiny legs on each side.
I move on the dirty ground.
I make no noise as I'm so small.
I am black and bumpy just like a trampoline.
You can find me in little, muddy tunnels
and I belong to a big family.
What am I?

Answer: A black ant.

Neitanas Miliauskis (7)
John Perry Primary School, Dagenham

What Am I?

I am bigger than a tiny ant
but I am smaller than a huge elephant.
I am wiggly on my wet, webbed leaves
and I love to get hot in the sun.
When I am happy, I wiggle.
When I feel the freezing water,
I come out soggy, as if I'm drenched in rain!
Some of my family are famous.
What am I?

Answer: A daisy.

Khairah Ahmed (7)
John Perry Primary School, Dagenham

Fluffy, Furry And Friendly

I am as fast as a sports car
zooming across the street.
Sometimes I am as slow as a sea snail.
I am as friendly as a giraffe.
Sometimes I gallop like a gazelle and horse.
I am browner than mud
on the hard, rocky ground.
I am as smooth as a pet hamster
in its metal cage.
What am I?

Answer: A moose.

Ibrahim Abdur-Rahman (7)
John Perry Primary School, Dagenham

Zap Zap

I am bigger than a red ant.
I am smaller than a grey elephant.
I flap my legs up and down
to go somewhere.
I zap like electricity when a wire is cut.
If you touch me, I'm really slimy.
Don't touch me or I will zap you!
If you run away, I will chase you.
What am I?

Answer: A jellyfish.

Daniel Adegoke (7)
John Perry Primary School, Dagenham

Big And Scary

I look fluffy, furry and brown.
I can be scary but sometimes I just
wander around and look after my cubs.
Sometimes I run fast or I might be slow.
I am quite loud and not silent.
My fur is as soft as a pillow
and it's very furry.
My fur is as soft as feathers.
What am I?

Answer: A bear.

Ava Olivia Phillips (6)
John Perry Primary School, Dagenham

Snap Snap

I am bigger than a mini ant but
I am smaller than a humongous giraffe.
I crawl on my dry feet.
When I want to eat people, I snap.
Snap, snap!
I am harder than a tortoise's shell and
I'm wet when I come out of the fresh water.
What am I?

Answer: A crocodile.

Kai Turner (7)
John Perry Primary School, Dagenham

What Am I?

I walk stealthily like a spy
through the green jungle.
I am an eating machine.
I viciously attack my prey.
I roar as loud as a lion.
When I'm in the jungle, I pounce on my prey.
I am caramel brown and yellow.
I sometimes eat people.
What am I?

Answer: A jaguar.

Alex Robert Dickens (7)
John Perry Primary School, Dagenham

What Am I?

I'm smaller than a huge elephant
but I'm bigger than a tiny ant.
I pounce for my prey on the large trees.
I purr when I'm happy
and I screech when I'm hungry.
I drink tasty milk with my spiky whiskers.
I drink milk on a plate.
What am I?

Answer: A cat.

Ekaterina Skolska (6)
John Perry Primary School, Dagenham

Fluffy Pets

I am slower than a leaping kangaroo
leaping like a wildcat.
Sometimes I land on people
and eat leaves most of the time.
I am colourful.
I am soft and silent.
I love people's gardens and flowers.
My tongue is a big, black line.
What am I?

Answer: A butterfly.

Chibumnuche Oprah-Gorgeous Eneremadu (7)
John Perry Primary School, Dagenham

Fluffy And Cute

I'm a furry pet to have.
If you have me, I am calm and slow
but sometimes I'm really fast and run quick.
I am sometimes friendly and full of peace.
My fur is soft and I am a great pet to have.
You can take me on a walk and stroke me.
What am I?

Answer: A cat.

Shazneen Haque (7)
John Perry Primary School, Dagenham

King Of The Ocean

I have razor-sharp teeth to eat my prey.
I am really frightening
and I sometimes eat people.
Sometimes my prey gets away but I never,
ever give up.
I swim in the sea, so mind out!
I am light grey and I eat fish.
What am I?

Answer: A shark.

Lewis Bivens (7)
John Perry Primary School, Dagenham

Predator

I am bigger than a teeny ant
but I am smaller than a giraffe.
I swim like a colourful fish.
I make loud sounds from far away.
I feel like I am drenched in rain!
Did you know I live in the shiny ocean?
What am I?

Answer: A killer whale.

Sara Beiene (6)
John Perry Primary School, Dagenham

Jump Jump

I am smaller than a huge, grey elephant
but I am bigger than a mini bee.
I jump on my dry feet when I'm happy.
When I'm smiling, I jump.
My fur is as brown as brown mud.
I have joeys in my pouch.
What am I?

Answer: A kangaroo.

Daniel Onyedikachukwu Obeigue (7)
John Perry Primary School, Dagenham

What Am I?

I am smaller than an elephant
but I'm bigger than an ant.
I hop and hop!
I crunch, crunch, crunch
and eat my crunchy carrots.
I am soft and as fluffy as my bed!
I have a friend called Peter.
What am I?

Answer: A rabbit.

Valerie Rua Gutierrez (6) & Victor
John Perry Primary School, Dagenham

Fluffy And Friendly

Sometimes I run as speedily
as a crazy cheetah.
I feel fluffy and cuddly.
I move briskly to eat fish and meat.
I look like a lion, brown and white.
I sound quieter than a horse noise.
I am a pet.
What am I?

Answer: A cat.

Shannon Thapa (7)
John Perry Primary School, Dagenham

The Cute And Fluffy

I am as playful as a toddler.
I am as happy as a baby.
I am as cute as a kitten.
I am as fast as a car.
I am as fluffy as a rabbit.
I am as noisy as a train.
I have blue eyes and brown fur.
What am I?

Answer: A puppy.

Mia Christie (6)
John Perry Primary School, Dagenham

What Am I?

I can run as fast as a racing car.
I am as soft as a pillow.
I am playful like a little girl at the park.
I am as cute as a baby.
I can be scary.
I sometimes drink milk.
I like to chase mice.
What am I?

Answer: A cat.

Madison Rose (7)
John Perry Primary School, Dagenham

A Soft Little Animal

I am cute when I want to play.
I am as fluffy as a rabbit.
I am very tiny when I am born.
I am as soft as a pillow.
I am as small as a ruler.
When my owners are gone,
I am mischevious.
What am I?

Answer: A kitten.

Melis Adan (7)
John Perry Primary School, Dagenham

Swishy Whoosh

I am bigger than a red car
and I am smaller than a tower.
In the wind, I shake my branches.
When it rains, I am as wet as a puddle.
I come out in the warm spring
but I die in winter.
What am I?

Answer: A blossom tree.

Brendan Bowen (7)
John Perry Primary School, Dagenham

The Smallest Animal

I am as fluffy as a coat.
I am as noisy as a baby.
Sometimes I am naughty but it's okay.
Sometimes I rest on a soft pillow.
I am as cute as a monkey.
Sometimes I'm unusual to people.
What am I?

Answer: A cat.

Keziah Pothin (8)
John Perry Primary School, Dagenham

Spotty

I am bigger than a tiny red ant,
and smaller than the moon.
I run all day until I get tired.
I bark as loud as a trumpet.
I am as furry as a rabbit.
I wag my tail when I'm excited.
What am I?

Answer: A dog.

Krystal Lacuna Bird (6)
John Perry Primary School, Dagenham

The Fast Animal

I am bigger than a tiny ant
but I am smaller than an elephant.
I am faster than a slow snail.
I neigh when I talk.
I am as smooth as marble.
My friend rides on me when she wants to.
What am I?

Answer: A horse.

Emily Maria Lungu (6)
John Perry Primary School, Dagenham

What Am I?

I am bigger than a spider
but I am smaller than a grey rhino.
I move silently and I've got hard, strong paws.
I roar like a speeding car engine.
I have orange and black stripes.
What am I?

Answer: A tiger.

Abdullah Burki (7)
John Perry Primary School, Dagenham

The Kindest Pet

I am as tiny as a mouse.
I am as naughty as a toddler.
I am as fast as a train.
I am as fast as all of the animals.
I am as soft as a cat.
I am as cute as a kitten.
What am I?

Answer: A cheetah.

Kian David Asamoah (6)
John Perry Primary School, Dagenham

The Fluffiest Animal

I am as fluffy as a pillow.
I am as white as a cloud.
I am as bouncy as a frog.
I am as soft as a teddy bear.
I am as cute as a newborn baby.
I am as smooth as paper.
What am I?

Answer: A bunny.

Alexandra Afolayan (7)
John Perry Primary School, Dagenham

What Am I?

I am bigger than a frog
and smaller than an elephant.
I run to chase my prey.
I roar when I am hungry.
When you try to hurt me, I will bite you
with my sharp teeth.
What am I?

Answer: A lion.

Michael Okinbaloye (7)
John Perry Primary School, Dagenham

As A Lovely Pet

I am as fluffy as can be.
People say I am cute.
I am as tiny as a toy.
I came from a cat's belly.
I am sometimes naughty.
I play with cotton balls.
What am I?

Answer: A kitten.

Nifemi Esho (6)
John Perry Primary School, Dagenham

The Cute Animal

I am as tiny as a mouse.
I am as fluffy as a cloud.
I am as fast as a cheetah.
I am as noisy as a train.
I am as funny as a toy.
I have blue eyes.
What am I?

Answer: A puppy.

Elze Zabulyte (7)
John Perry Primary School, Dagenham

Always Aggressive

I am as fast as a car and a cheetah.
I am always aggressive.
I have a little tail.
I have fat legs.
I am always grumpy.
I have short ears.
What am I?

Answer: A rhino.

Ronnie Peter Keith Bland (7)
John Perry Primary School, Dagenham

Jumpy And Kind

I am as fast as a cheetah.
My skin is very furry.
I am active.
I am very loud.
I am very jumpy.
I am annoying.
I am very cheeky.
What am I?

Answer: A monkey.

Rdwan Montasir (6)
John Perry Primary School, Dagenham

Super Flash

I am golden.
I am as fast as a cheetah.
I am as cute as a baby.
I like to be tickled on my tummy.
I am as soft as a baby lion.
What am I?

Answer: A dog.

Ifechukwu Joshua Anuna (6)
John Perry Primary School, Dagenham

What Is He?

He lives in Africa.
He is big.
He is brown.
He has four legs.
He has two big ears.
What is he?

Answer: An elephant.

Samuel Elijah (7)
John Perry Primary School, Dagenham

I Can Fly

I am as black as charcoal.
I am fast like a car.
I am scary.
I eat frogs.
I am blind.
What am I?

Answer: A bat.

Ronnie Spence (7)
John Perry Primary School, Dagenham

What Are They?

They smell like dandelions and raspberries.
The sunlight goes onto them.
When the wind blows, it is like this,
swish, swish!
When it rains, the water goes
into their roots.
Every day they grow bigger and bigger.
They are a hundred years old.
Some are different like a rainbow in the sky.
Some have pollen and blossom.
They have brown stuff inside
and one is dark red.
What are they?

Answer: A daffodil and a rose.

Spencer Garcia (6)
Newtons Primary School, Rainham

What Am I?

I have ginger spots on me
and white on the rest.
I eat meat and tuna.
I love food.
I am still a baby.
I am always at home
because I get lost outside.
I am small because I am a baby.
I am very cute, cuddly and fluffy.
I stay in a box full of blankets and pillows
with milk and food.
I am not allowed to eat chocolate
because it poisons me.
What am I?

Answer: A cat.

Ruby Reed (6)
Newtons Primary School, Rainham

Fast Spotter

I am as fast as a tiger.
I am yellow and black.
I live in the desert.
I run a hundred miles per hour.
I eat birds.
I am not really friendly and I fight.
I've got sharp teeth.
I jump high.
I bite really hard.
I've got a really long tail.
I am very spotty.
What am I?

Answer: A cheetah.

Anton Gabriel (5)
Newtons Primary School, Rainham

What Am I?

I am ginger and white.
I have sharp claws and teeth.
I have blue eyes.
I have a long, curly tail.
I am soft, furry and cuddly.
I am a baby animal.
I am so lovely.
I have lungs to breathe.
I drink milk.
I am a mammal.
I have four legs.
I poo and wee outside.
What am I?

Answer: A kitten.

Ellie Wicks (6)
Newtons Primary School, Rainham

What Am I?

I am as pink as a T-shirt.
I like to munch and crunch on carrots.
I squeak because I'm happy.
Please be kind and stroke and cuddle me.
I like yellow, straight hay.
I eat honey biscuits.
What am I?

Answer: A guinea pig.

Robert John Wisbey (6)
Newtons Primary School, Rainham

Rainbow Rainbow

I have long, black legs.
I have pointy, black ears.
I have a grumpy face all day.
I have a black tail.
I eat meat because I am a carnivore.
I have black fur all over my body.
What am I?

Answer: A dog.

Max Turner (6)
Newtons Primary School, Rainham

Pretty Rainbows

I have a pretty horn.
I eat cake.
My hair is pretty like a rainbow.
I love rainbows when they have lots of colours.
I live in Heaven.
I have wings like a butterfly.
What am I?

Answer: A unicorn.

Grace Gibbons (6)
Newtons Primary School, Rainham

What Is It?

It has a flower on it.
It is hard and it has the sunshine on it.
It is not alive.
It has a back but it isn't a person.
It stands on the grass but it's not a person.
What is it?

Answer: A chair.

Lillie Davenport (5)
Newtons Primary School, Rainham

Splashy Friendly

I have tusks.
I have a dirty tail.
I get water to splash other animals.
That's right, I am splash-friendly!
I have two 'E's in my name.
I am not a toy.
What am I?

Answer: An elephant.

Rehnuma Tajrin (5)
Newtons Primary School, Rainham

Sparkles

I am shiny.
I have smooth stuff on me.
I am red and purple, also blue.
I am living underground.
I am glittery and sparkly in the night.
I glow in the night.
What am I?

Answer: A crystal.

Zara Kasule (6)
Newtons Primary School, Rainham

Fluffy Ball

I am as small as an apple.
I am all different colours.
I run very fast and I fit in small places.
I look like a little furry ball.
I eat grass and I am a pet.
What am I?

Answer: A guinea pig.

Laila Tonto (6)
Newtons Primary School, Rainham

What Am I?

I have little black hairs.
I have really strong wings.
I have sharp teeth and ears.
I have red eyes.
I am scruffy.
I am mean.
I have dark grey hair.
What am I?

Answer: A bat.

James Hammond (6)
Newtons Primary School, Rainham

Hisss

I have no legs.
I slither along.
My body is covered in scales.
I can be very short or very long.
My tongue is fork-shaped.
I like to wrap around trees.
What am I?

Answer: A snake.

Alfie Feasey (6)
Newtons Primary School, Rainham

Cutie

I have fluffy, soft fur.
I have claws like a tiger.
I have sharp teeth and a tail.
I have four strong legs.
I eat meat.
I have three thin whiskers.
What am I?

Answer: A cat.

William Mason (6)
Newtons Primary School, Rainham

Snowball

When I am happy, I purr.
I drink milk and I like to eat tuna.
I am as white as snow.
I sleep in the day.
I can scratch you when I'm angry.
What am I?

Answer: A cat.

Lilly-Rose Bailey (5)
Newtons Primary School, Rainham

I Am Soft

I am soft and cute.
I am a mammal.
I drink milk.
I play with toys.
I have black fur all over my body.
I miaow when I want something.
What am I?

Answer: A cat.

Naya Garcia-Clegg (5)
Newtons Primary School, Rainham

What Am I?

I have orange and black stripes.
I have sharp claws.
I live in the long jungle.
I have a yellow tail.
I am a mammal.
I eat meat.
What am I?

Answer: A tiger.

Bobby Potter (6)
Newtons Primary School, Rainham

What Am I?

I like red apples and yellow hay.
I have got four legs to run very fast.
I like to munch on green grass.
You can ride me.
What am I?

Answer: A horse.

Kiah Morris (6)
Newtons Primary School, Rainham

What Am I?

I am a brown milk drinker.
My tail is very short.
I have whiskers that are really long.
I am as furry as a polar bear.
What am I?

Answer: A cat.

Amy Rodriguez-Ahmed (6)
Newtons Primary School, Rainham

It's A Hop

I take your carrots and poop.
I have babies.
When I eat your carrots, I take my teeth out.
I like to jump and hop.
What am I?

Answer: A rabbit.

Rabiah Azhar (5)
Newtons Primary School, Rainham

Big Hoppy

I have long ears to listen.
I like carrots to eat.
My tail is fluffy.
I poo outside.
I love to hop and jump.
What am I?

Answer: A rabbit.

Samanta Smeiksta (5)
Newtons Primary School, Rainham

The Swinger

I am brown like chocolate.
I have big ears like an elephant.
I am very cheeky.
My tail is long like a sausage.
What am I?

Answer: A monkey.

Bailey George Kreuder (6)
Newtons Primary School, Rainham

What Am I?

I have black fur.
I drink milk.
I jump on the toys.
I shout.
I sleep on the bed.
I chase fish.
What am I?

Answer: A cat.

Jay-J Gardiner (5)
Newtons Primary School, Rainham

What Am I?

I have black fur.
I drink milk and eat meat.
I have long whiskers.
I can jump over the fence.
What am I?

Answer: A cat.

Katie Davenport (5)
Newtons Primary School, Rainham

Fluffy Cute

My animal is so cute and fluffy.
It is really, really cheeky.
It is really small and kind.
What is it?

Answer: A puppy.

Lilly-Rose Persia Akbari (6)
Newtons Primary School, Rainham

What Is It?

It has big ears.
It is grey.
Also, it has tusks.
What is it?

Answer: An elephant.

Amber Debenham (5)
Newtons Primary School, Rainham

What Am I?

I have yellow fur.
I eat meat.
I sleep in the sun.
What am I?

Answer: A lion.

Bryan Buttery (6)
Newtons Primary School, Rainham

The Night Hunter

I am a special and unusual bird of prey
with orange eyes and I'm a silent hunter.
My spinning head spins around for a
long time to show what I am looking for.
I have fierce, strong teeth.
I make a loud hooting noise in the night
and I have feathers like a pillow.
When I find my prey, I fly down like a
swooping diver and eat it with my fierce,
strong teeth.
When I am ravenous, I will gobble up mice
for lunch using my claws to grab it.
If other animals try to eat me, it won't work
because I have super sharp claws.
What am I?

Answer: An owl.

Nifise Femi-Sanni (7)
Whybridge Infant School, Rainham

Multicoloured

I am pretty and I am multicoloured.
I am really skinny and I have a beak.
I eat insects.
My wings are really wide and
my feet are orange, like duck feet.
I have got long lashes like a camel.
I am really stripy.
My wings can come out wide
and they are really multicoloured.
I have loads of patterns.
I have got blue, yellow, pink
and green feathers.
What am I?

Answer: A peacock.

Elsie-Lennox Morgan (7)
Whybridge Infant School, Rainham

Africa

I am a bit furry.
I've got tiny ears
so I can hear things properly.
I am yellow and I have a long neck
so I can reach tall things.
My four legs are a bit long.
My big head is shorter than a pillow.
The place I live is Africa and I have
a small tail and I eat trees.
My furry, yellow skin has black spots
but I still have yellow skin.
What am I?

Answer: A giraffe.

Kirsten Asante (6)
Whybridge Infant School, Rainham

The Mammal That Lays Eggs

I am an unusual mammal because
I have body parts like other animals.
When something tries to eat me,
I'll sting them with my venomous spur.
My babies hatch out of eggs.
My tail is like a beaver's tail,
which is flat and strong.
I use my webbed feet to swim gracefully.
When there is prey around,
catch it with my bill.
What am I?

Answer: A platypus.

Tiana Tu (7)
Whybridge Infant School, Rainham

Multicoloured Mayhem

I have big eyes and hang upside down.
There are not many animals like me.
I am really good at camouflaging in trees.
When I am in a mood, I change colour.
Not many reptiles are like me.
The colours on me make me look poisonous so don't eat me!
My feet can grip so I don't fall off trees.
What am I?

Answer: A chameleon.

Jessica Denise Middleton Marden (7)
Whybridge Infant School, Rainham

High Flyer

My venomous teeth will kill you
if you annoy me.
If I see some prey, I fly high in the sky
and I swoop down to catch it.
When something is trying to attack me,
I camouflage in bushes.
I've got a poisonous tail that is very long.
I can also make my tail curl up
and hang upside down.
What am I?

Answer: A dragon.

Noah Ashaley Leach (7)
Whybridge Infant School, Rainham

The Red Breather

I breathe fire like the burning sun.
I have four legs and I'm scary.
When I'm hungry, I eat meat from people.
If I'm annoyed, I will breathe fire at you.
I can fly and I have scales.
If I have prey in front of me, I will hide
by flying in the sky and I'll dive and eat it.
What am I?

Answer: A dragon.

Dovydas Zilionis (6)
Whybridge Infant School, Rainham

Travelling Man

I wear red and white and
I am in a fictional book.
I have a friend called Wenda
and a dog called Woof.
I have got some glasses and a bobble hat.
My arch nemesis is called Odlaw.
I travel around the world and hide.
Children love my books and
I am very tricky to find.
Who am I?

Answer: Where's Wally?

Declan Armstrong-Smith (7)
Whybridge Infant School, Rainham

Minibeasts

I am poisonous and little.
I can climb up trees and I walk slowly.
Sometimes I'm mean because I'm hairy.
I eat leaves to grow.
I have legs on the bottom.
On my legs, I have tiny spikes.
I am green and orange.
When I'm older, I'll grow wings and fly.
What am I?

Answer: A caterpillar.

Seyi Odukaya (7)
Whybridge Infant School, Rainham

The Tropical Scales

My babies are extremely heavy.
I live on a tropical island which is really nice.
My body is covered in black scales.
My eggs are extremely big.
If I eat you with my venomous teeth,
it will be really painful.
I have scales but I go on the ground
and in the water.
What am I?

Answer: A Komodo dragon.

Bobby Fletcher (7)
Whybridge Infant School, Rainham

What Am I?

I have venomous, sharp teeth
because I am a carnivore.
When I'm hungry,
I will catch you with my talons.
My baby will hatch next to the volcano
with my family.
If I'm mad, I will breathe horrifying sun fire.
I have got a long tail but I'm not a crow.
What am I?

Answer: A dragon.

Yasir Uddin (7)
Whybridge Infant School, Rainham

Jungle Animal

I am black and orange.
I am fluffy and I look for my prey.
I blend in with the grass and hay
and sneak up on my prey.
My tail is very soft like a dog.
I run very fast to catch my prey.
I have four legs, not two.
I have no owner because I live in the wild.
What am I?

Answer: A tiger.

Kaden Sydes (7)
Whybridge Infant School, Rainham

Who Am I?

I am a gem lover.
I am nice and cute.
I like to walk in the woods
but I have animals instead of friends.
I have a pink, puffy dress.
I have luxurious, blonde hair and blue eyes.
Did you know I have shiny shoes
with diamonds?
Who am I?

Answer: Princess Peach.

Richard Bogdan Gavrau (6)
Whybridge Infant School, Rainham

Swing Through The Rainforest

I am brown and I swing in trees.
I throw banana peels on the floor.
I live in the rainforest.
I have a long tail to help me climb trees, it's like an extra arm.
I eat bananas and animals.
I eat upside down and have lots of hair.
What am I?

Answer: A monkey.

Liam Breavington (6)
Whybridge Infant School, Rainham

Writing

I come from a factory.
I have loads of pictures inside.
I am white, black and red all over.
I am not food and I am not alive.
In the factory, I get writing put on me.
If you need me, you need to go
to the shop and buy me.
What am I?

Answer: A newspaper.

Ellie Cox (6)
Whybridge Infant School, Rainham

The Flying Monster

I have a scaly body and it is really smooth.
When someone annoys me, I eat them!
I have venomous teeth that can kill you.
If I come to your house, I will burn it.
I have hot breathing fire that is boiling hot.
I am always angry.
What am I?

Answer: A dragon.

Marta Jurga (7)
Whybridge Infant School, Rainham

The Slow Rider

I have bumps on my back.
I can stay awake until morning.
I don't eat for twenty-eight miles.
My eyelashes keep sand out of my eyes.
I live in the desert.
You might be sick because
the lump in my back is very bumpy.
What am I?

Answer: A camel.

Ekisha Kaiza (7)
Whybridge Infant School, Rainham

African Animals

I have small ears and a long tail.
I am huge and I am furry.
I have brown spots and I am yellow.
My neck is really long and I am an animal.
I have a big tummy and I live in Africa.
I have little eyes and I like leaves.
What am I?

Answer: A giraffe.

Katie Weston-Lucas (7)
Whybridge Infant School, Rainham

The Speed Beast

I am a master of speed.
When I am a beast, I can kill people.
I have no feet but round things.
I make an enormous noise,
an extremely big noise.
I am the fastest object in the land.
I was made in Italy.
What am I?

Answer: A Lamborghini.

Albos Dega (7)
Whybridge Infant School, Rainham

It's Time To Get Real

I am grumpy and angry.
I am lazy.
I have long whiskers and black stripes.
I hate my brother Odie because he is a dog.
I am always grumpy, especially on Mondays.
My owner's friend always drives a flying car.
Who am I?

Answer: Garfield.

Vinny Joseph Kerrigan (7)
Whybridge Infant School, Rainham

Fierce Fish

I am a predator and I have no legs.
I live in Australia and
I have really sharp teeth.
My skin is smooth and I am really sly.
My favourite food is big fish and small fish.
I swim really fast and I eat people.
What am I?

Answer: A shark.

Jack Barry (7)
Whybridge Infant School, Rainham

The Fast Runner

I am an animal that has black stripes.
I have an orange body and a loud sound.
My body is so big and I run fast.
When I move off my stone, I get my food.
I go to find something to eat.
I live in the jungle.
What am I?

Answer: A tiger.

Hollie Hartley (7)
Whybridge Infant School, Rainham

The Snappy

I have really sharp teeth.
I can go on land and sea.
My tail is as long as two layers of people.
I am as slimy as a jellyfish.
I have a snappy mouth.
I can crawl because I have little legs.
What am I?

Answer: A crocodile.

Connor Mason Ross (7)
Whybridge Infant School, Rainham

The Silent Bird

I have little feathers.
When I twist my head, it does not hurt.
I swoop down to catch my prey.
My eyes are orange and big.
I fly silently with my wings.
I make weird noises in the trees.
What am I?

Answer: An owl.

Aironas Astrauskas (7)
Whybridge Infant School, Rainham

The Big Beast

I can climb trees very high up.
My tail is softer than a pillow.
I am brave, big and strong.
I am good at running faster than a lion.
I am always hunting for food.
My teeth are sharp.
What am I?

Answer: A jaguar.

Mia Ramanauskaite (7)
Whybridge Infant School, Rainham

The Slither Beast

I have black and brown scales.
My tongue is red and short.
I am very long and thin.
My skin is very bumpy and smooth.
My tongue is forked and very sharp.
My eyes are small and brown.
What am I?

Answer: A snake.

Jonny Melhuish (7)
Whybridge Infant School, Rainham

Patchy And Fast

I am horrid and annoying to my owner
but I like her really.
I am an attacker and I don't like people.
I have sharp claws.
I have brown fur so I can blend in
with rocks.
What am I?

Answer: A leopard.

Honey-Blue Donoghue (6)
Whybridge Infant School, Rainham

My Favourite Food

I have a sausage in me.
I have mustard and ketchup on top of me.
You might want onions with me.
My bun is very soft.
You eat me with your hands.
You can get me at school.
What am I?

Answer: A hot dog.

Jake Flatt (7)
Whybridge Infant School, Rainham

Amazing Technicolor

This is a certain type of bird
but it's not a hawk.
He sits on a pirate's shoulder while
letting out a squawk.
He says that he's a carrot but he's actually...
What is he?

Answer: A parrot.

Ethan Micheal Clifton (7)
Whybridge Infant School, Rainham

A Lion King

I have a furry mane.
I have sharp, shiny teeth
and little, fluffy ears.
I hunt for food.
I am the king of the jungle.
I have long whiskers and furry paws
like a cat.
What am I?

Answer: A lion.

Solange Danso (7)
Whybridge Infant School, Rainham

The Silvery Beast

I can slither on the ground.
I am really scaly.
When you come near me, I will eat you.
My tongue is really poisonous.
My skin is smooth.
I camouflage in the desert.
What am I?

Answer: A snake.

Luca Greenspan (6)
Whybridge Infant School, Rainham

Bouncy Animal

I have a pouch and I live in Australia.
I am very dangerous when I kick.
I can jump high.
I am sly and cute.
I am kind.
I am like a hare or a rabbit but bigger.
What am I?

Answer: A kangaroo.

Caiden Sita (6)
Whybridge Infant School, Rainham

The Flame Thrower

I have scaly, red scales.
I can breathe smoking orange fire.
I am fearless and scary.
My roar is loud and scary.
I have deep red wings.
My eyes are dark green.
What am I?

Answer: A dragon.

Charlie Harris (7)
Whybridge Infant School, Rainham

The Delicious Red

I am yummy.
I am red.
My juice is nice and tasty.
I have small seeds.
People put sugar and melted chocolate on me.
I am in the shop with other fruit.
What am I?

Answer: A strawberry.

Teddy Snee (6)
Whybridge Infant School, Rainham

Super Fast Car

I am very loud and have rainbow colours.
I have bright wheels.
I have a logo starting with an 'L'.
I have two boosters at the back.
My seats are blue.
What am I?

Answer: A Lamborghini.

Altay Kocak (7)
Whybridge Infant School, Rainham

Fruit

I am heavy and juicy.
I have black seeds and I am red.
My bottom is green.
I am a fruit.
You can have me for lunch.
I am cold and taste nice.
What am I?

Answer: A watermelon.

Ioana Dainty (7)
Whybridge Infant School, Rainham

The Mean Croc

I am shiny, green and mean.
I am soaking wet.
My skin is really scaly.
I have sharp teeth.
I am incredibly mean.
My tail is long and scary.
What am I?

Answer: An alligator.

Leo Foster (7)
Whybridge Infant School, Rainham

Fruity Looty

I am red.
I have small pips.
I have green, teeny tiny leaves.
You can eat me if you want to.
I come from a plant.
You can dip me in sugar.
What am I?

Answer: A strawberry.

Olivia Jackson (7)
Whybridge Infant School, Rainham

The Seedy Bun

I come from a cow.
I am tasty.
I have a bun.
I have onion.
My ketchup is really, really yummy.
I come from cafes and fast food places.
What am I?

Answer: A hamburger.

Georgia Turner (7)
Whybridge Infant School, Rainham

The Hot Man

I am tasty.
There is a sausage inside of me.
You can eat me.
My best friend is bread.
I have mustard on my body.
My colour is red.
What am I?

Answer: A hot dog.

Dilanas Bogusa (7)
Whybridge Infant School, Rainham

River Monster

I live in a river and swim all day.
I cannot walk because I have no legs.
I can breathe underwater.
I can swim with my tail and flap my fins.
What am I?

Answer: A fish.

Nikola Bojdzińska (7)
Whybridge Infant School, Rainham

The Yummiest Thing On Earth

I am yummy.
You use your hands to eat me.
I am sold in a wrapper.
You open me with excitement.
You enjoy me with fries.
What am I?

Answer: A cheeseburger.

Simon Olabisi (7)
Whybridge Infant School, Rainham

High Sky

I am a vegetarian.
I like to jump high in the sky.
My ears are long.
My colour is any colour.
I am as soft as silk.
What am I?

Answer: A bunny.

Joan Ukpokolo (7)
Whybridge Infant School, Rainham

Desert Animal

I live in the desert.
I have long eyelashes.
I can walk for miles.
I can carry people or luggage.
I live in Africa.
What am I?

Answer: A camel.

Jake Charlie Tony Walker (6)
Whybridge Infant School, Rainham

Stripes

I have stripes.
I live on a farm.
My body is stripy.
My body is relaxed.
I live in a desert.
What am I?

Answer: A zebra.

Kaiden Linford-Mehmet (7)
Whybridge Infant School, Rainham

Wild

You can hop on my saddle.
I have four legs and I am brown.
I am fast and big.
I have big ears.
What am I?

Answer: A horse.

Riley Chuch (7)
Whybridge Infant School, Rainham

Beautiful And Colourful

I am a rainbow with bright colours.
My tongue is long.
I eat flies.
What am I?

Answer: A rainbow tree frog.

Izhonia Romewun Pearl Agbaje (6)
Whybridge Infant School, Rainham

YoungWriters
Est.1991

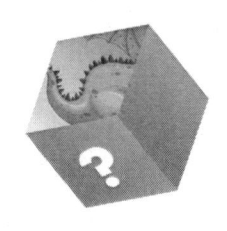

YOUNG WRITERS INFORMATION

We hope you have enjoyed reading this book – and that you will continue to in the coming years.

If you're a young writer who enjoys reading and creative writing, or the parent of an enthusiastic poet or story writer, do visit our website **www.youngwriters.co.uk**. Here you will find free competitions, workshops and games, as well as recommended reads, a poetry glossary and our blog.

If you would like to order further copies of this book, or any of our other titles, then please give us a call or visit **www.youngwriters.co.uk**.

Young Writers
Remus House
Coltsfoot Drive
Peterborough
PE2 9BF
(01733) 890066
info@youngwriters.co.uk